Structuring Success

A Simple Guide To Growing

Your Small Business

Written By: Brent & Tamela

Copyright © 2025 by Brent & Tamela

All rights reserved.

No part of this publication may be reproduced, distributed, or transmitted in any form or by any means, including photocopying, recording, or other electronic or mechanical methods, without the prior written permission of the publisher, except as permitted by U.S. copyright law.

The story, all names, characters, and incidents portrayed in this production are fictitious. No identification with actual persons (living or deceased), places, buildings, and products is intended or should be inferred.

ISBN: 9798303044371

DISCLAIMER: The information provided in this book is for informational purposes only and is not intended to be a source of advice or credit analysis with respect to the material presented. The information and/or documents contained in this book do not constitute legal or financial advice and should never be used without first consulting with a financial professional to determine what may be best for your individual needs.

The publisher and the author do not make any guarantee or other promise as to any results that may be obtained from using the content of this book. You should never make any investment decision without first consulting with your own financial advisor and conducting your own research and due diligence. To the maximum extent permitted by law, the publisher and the author disclaim any and all liability in the event any information, commentary, analysis, opinions, advice and/or recommendations contained in this book prove to be inaccurate, incomplete or unreliable, or result in any investment or other losses.

Content contained or made available through this book is not intended to and does not constitute legal advice or investment advice and no attorney-client relationship is formed. The publisher and the author are providing this book and its contents on an "as is" basis. Your use of the information in this book is at your own risk.

Although the publisher and the author have made every effort to ensure that the information in this book was correct at press time and while this publication is designed to provide accurate information in regard to the subject matter covered, the publisher and the author assume no responsibility for errors, inaccuracies, omissions, or any other inconsistencies herein and hereby disclaim any liability to any party for any loss, damage, or disruption caused by errors or omissions, whether such errors or omissions result from negligence, accident, or any other cause.

This publication is meant as a source of valuable information for the reader, however it is not meant as a substitute for direct expert assistance. If such a level of assistance is required, the services of a competent professional should be sought.

Table of Contents

Introduction 2

Step 1: Crafting a Strong Operating Agreement 5

Step 2: Choosing the Right Management Structure 14

Step 3: Financial Foundations 20

Step 4: Borrowing Money 29

Step 5: Building a Strong Team 38

Step 6: Marketing and Branding 47

Conclusion 52

Dedication

This book is dedicated to the extraordinary teams of hardworking souls who have poured their passion and dedication into the journey of our businesses.

To the late nights and early mornings, to the countless meetings and brainstorming sessions, your tireless efforts have sculpted the foundation upon which our ventures stand tall. You are not just employees; you are the architects of all that has been accomplished.

In every project completed, every goal surpassed, and every milestone reached, it is your dedication that has made the difference.

Thank you for being the heartbeat of our businesses.

Colossians 3:23

And whatsoever ye do, do it heartily, as to the Lord, and not unto men;

With deepest gratitude,

Brent & Tamela

Introduction

Running a small business is a complex endeavor and there are several challenges that can make it feel overwhelming. First off, small businesses often have limited resources and a small team, so decisions about where to spend money need careful consideration. People working in small businesses usually have to do many different jobs, like marketing and handling finances. Just following all the rules and laws at local, state, and national levels can be scary and failing to do so can lead to legal trouble. Staying competitive will most certainly require constant creativity and a thorough understanding of what customers want.

Managing money flow is crucial, and not doing so will cause financial problems. This requires using technology, planning for risks, and thinking ahead for growth. According to the U.S. Bureau of Labor Statistics (BLS), about 20% of new businesses fail during the first two years of being open, 45% during the first five years, and 65% during the first 10 years. This extremely high failure rate can be almost entirely attributed to inadequate capital or poor management. This includes a lack of business planning, poor decision-making, and inadequate leadership.

Tamela and I have weathered the storms of entrepreneurship, navigated the highs and lows, and emerged stronger, wiser, and more successful than ever. In the early days, we faced our fair share of challenges. Starting from scratch, we built our empire step by step, learning the ropes of the business world through sheer determination. Success didn't come overnight, but with each hurdle, we refined our skills and embraced the lessons that came our way.

We've found success through a number of ventures including an information technology company, a thriving marketing firm, a savvy real estate investment business, a Top 100 roofing company, a residential home construction company, and an import business. It's a diverse portfolio that mirrors our passion for exploring new territories and challenging the status quo.

What truly sets us apart is not a list of successful businesses but the heart and soul we've poured into each one. It's not about titles or accolades; it's about the journey, the joy of overcoming obstacles, and the satisfaction of seeing our hard work pay off.

Sure, we've achieved success, but we're not ones to rest on our laurels. We approach every venture with a humble mindset, acknowledging that there's always room for improvement. The secret sauce? A blend of expertise, a shared vision, and a good dose of humor. Because, let's face it, the business world can be intense, and sometimes we just have to stop and laugh.

So, step into our world, where success is a mix of hard work, humility, and a sprinkle of fun. Brent and Tamela – a couple who've not only weathered the storms but learned to dance in the rain, turning every challenge into an opportunity for growth. It's a journey we're proud of, and we can't wait to help you reach your business goals.

We'll help you understand the ins and outs of making your business thrive. We'll look at different ways to manage a team and break down the pros and cons of each approach. If you're diving into the world of LLCs, we've got you covered on the importance of a strong operating agreement. We'll walk you through the key things you need to include and how to make it fit your business.

We'll also tackle the financial side of things. Setting up a strong financial foundation, budgeting, and understanding financial planning which is absolutely crucial for your business success. Plus, we'll explore different ways to borrow money, like loans, grants, and investors, giving you tips on building a solid credit profile.

We truly want to see you succeed and enjoy all the blessings that are available to us in this amazing country!

Step 1:
Crafting a Strong Operating Agreement

CASE STUDY:

Two friends, Jake and Mike, shared a passion for fixing cars. Eager to turn their expertise into a thriving business, they opened "GearWorks Garage" with dreams of becoming the go-to auto repair shop in town. Little did they know that the absence of a strong operating agreement would put their venture on a collision course with failure.

In the early days, GearWorks Garage was a hub of activity. The duo's skills attracted a steady stream of customers seeking reliable car repairs. As the business flourished, so did the strains on Jake and Mike's friendship. Without a clear operating agreement, issues related to workload, profit-sharing, and decision-making festered beneath the surface.

As GearWorks Garage expanded its services, the lack of a structured agreement became evident. Jake believed they should invest in new diagnostic equipment to stay competitive, while Mike preferred sticking to their current tools to maximize short-term profits. Disagreements on major business decisions intensified, creating a rift between the once-united partners.

Trouble escalated when Jake wanted to bring in a third mechanic to handle the increasing workload, while Mike was resistant to the idea. The absence of guidelines for expanding the team and responsibilities further strained their relationship. Frustrations reached a boiling point, leading to a fallout between the co-owners.

The breaking point came when a high-profile customer's vintage car suffered damage during repairs. Without a predefined process for handling customer disputes, Jake and Mike found themselves in a heated argument. The customer ultimately left dissatisfied, and negative reviews began to tarnish GearWorks Garage's reputation.

As the dispute escalated, the lack of a clear exit strategy in their operating agreement left both Jake and Mike facing financial hardships. Legal battles ensued, and GearWorks Garage, once a symbol of their shared dream, faced closure. Customers witnessed the downfall of a once-thriving auto repair shop, and the town mourned the loss of GearWorks Garage.

The story of GearWorks Garage is a reminder of the importance of a well-structured operating agreement. The absence of this foundational document led to the demise of a promising auto repair shop, leaving behind a lesson etched in the grease-stained memories of the two entrepreneurs.

Running a business can be exciting, but without a clear plan, things can get messy. Imagine your business as a ship—its success depends on a well-drawn map. That's where an operating agreement comes in. Whether you're sailing solo or have a team, having a solid agreement is like having a reliable compass, guiding you through challenges and uncertainties.

Many business owners are aware that they should have a written business plan but don't understand the importance of an operating agreement. So, how is an operating agreement different from a business plan? The operating agreement is like an internal handbook for Limited Liability Companies (LLCs). It talks about how things work inside the company – who does what, how profits are shared, and how conflicts are sorted out. It's a set of rules for the members of the LLC, and it's legally binding. Think of it as the team playbook.

On the other hand, a business plan is like a big picture guide for the entire business. It covers everything from what the business is about, who the customers are, and how it plans to make money. Unlike the operating agreement, the business plan isn't a rulebook, and it's not legally binding. It's more like a story you tell to outside people – investors, lenders, or potential partners. It's meant to attract support and investment by showing where the business is headed.

So, the operating agreement is like an internal playbook for the team, while the business plan is an external story for the outside world. Each has its own role in making sure your business runs smoothly and grows successfully.

Let's break it down. Even if you're the only member, having a written agreement is crucial. It spells out who's in charge, how profits and losses are handled, and how decisions are made. Think of it as the user manual for your business.

For a solo entrepreneur, the agreement helps protect your personal stuff—like your car or house—from any business-related messes. It draws a clear line between your personal life and your business, keeping your personal assets safe.

For businesses with multiple members, the agreement avoids headaches by clearly stating who does what and who gets what. It's your insurance against misunderstandings and conflicts, providing a clear path for resolving disputes before they become major problems.

Every business is unique, and your operating agreement should reflect that. It's not a one-size-fits-all document. You get to customize it to fit your business's specific needs. From how decisions are made to how profits are split, it's all in your hands. This flexibility ensures that your business rules match your vision.

Besides being your business's rulebook, the operating agreement also makes sure you're following the law. It outlines the structure of your business, who's involved, and how things are run. This legal paperwork isn't just for show—it's what makes your business official and helps you stay on the right side of the law.

Businesses aren't static; they change and grow. A good operating agreement is ready for that. If you want to bring in a new partner, change how profits are split, or tweak any other detail, you can do that. It's your business's way of saying, "I'm ready for whatever comes next."

In simple terms, your operating agreement is like a superhero cape for your business. It shields you from personal liability, keeps things clear and organized, and adapts as your business evolves. Whether you're a lone ranger or part of a team, investing time in creating a solid operating agreement is an investment in the smooth sailing and long-term success of your business. It's not just paperwork, it's your business's trusted guide.

CASE STUDY:

Alex, Lisa, and Michael — embarked on a journey to establish a manufacturing company specializing in eco-friendly packaging solutions. United by their passion for sustainability, they founded "GreenPac Manufacturing." However, the absence of a robust operating agreement cast a shadow on their dream, particularly when the time came to sell their company.

GreenPac Manufacturing started strong, becoming a pioneer in sustainable packaging. As the factory flourished, so did the complexities of managing the business. Decisions about market expansion, production strategies, and financial investments became pivotal. The absence of a clear operating agreement allowed differences in opinions on these matters to fester among the siblings, creating tension within the family.

When the opportunity to sell GreenPac arose, the absence of provisions for selling the business became glaringly evident. Disagreements over the sale terms, valuation, and distribution of proceeds ensued, leaving the siblings in a challenging predicament. The lack of a predetermined process for handling such a significant decision strained family relationships and jeopardized the potential success of the sale.

External factors added to the turmoil. Prospective buyers, sensing the internal discord, exploited the lack of cohesion among the siblings during negotiations. The absence of a united front allowed the potential buyers to dictate terms that favored their interests, leaving the siblings with less than they had hoped for.

As the sale process unfolded, the absence of a strong operating agreement left the siblings facing both financial setbacks and strained family ties.

Family-owned businesses are at a higher risk of facing problems when they don't have a strong operating agreement. The close ties and history within a family generally create assumptions about roles and decisions, leading to misunderstandings. If your family run business doesn't have a strong operating agreement this should be a priority.

An operating agreement can vary depending on the business and what its members want, but there are some important things that are usually part of most operating agreements. Here's a list of key elements that you'll often find in an operating agreement:

1. Business Basics:
    - Name of the LLC.
    - Formation date.
    - Location of the principal place of business.
2. Members' Information:
    - Names and addresses of all members.
    - Percentage of ownership or membership interest of each member.

3. Management Structure:
   - Specify whether the LLC will be member-managed or manager-managed.
   - If manager-managed, detail the roles and responsibilities of managers.

4. Capital Contributions:
   - Outline the initial contributions made by each member to the LLC.
   - Specify how additional capital contributions will be handled.

5. Profit and Loss Allocation:
   - Describe how profits and losses will be allocated among members.
   - Outline the distribution of profits, if any.

6. Decision-Making and Voting:
   - Establish the decision-making process for significant business matters.
   - Specify voting rights and procedures for member meetings.

7. Transfer of Membership Interests:
   - Outline restrictions on the transfer of membership interests.
   - Specify the process for approving or disapproving transfers.

8. Dissolution:

    - Establish the procedures for dissolving the LLC, including voting requirements.

9. Dispute Resolution:

    - Include mechanisms for resolving disputes among members.
    - Specify whether mediation, arbitration, or litigation will be used.

10. Buy-Sell Provisions:

    - Detailed procedures for the sale of a member's interest, including triggering events.
    - Establish the valuation method for determining the price of a member's interest.

11. Succession Planning:

    - Address what happens in the event of a member's death, incapacity, or withdrawal.
    - Specify how the deceased or withdrawing member's interest will be handled.

12. Amendments to the Operating Agreement:

    - Outline the process for amending the operating agreement.
    - Typically requires the consent of a certain percentage of members.

Imagine your operating agreement as the instruction manual for your business game. It's like sitting down with your team and setting some ground rules. First things first, figure out who's in charge—are decisions made together, or is there a captain? Then, chat about the money side of things—what's everyone putting in, and how are the profits going to be divided up? It's also good to talk about what happens if someone decides to leave or if you need to make changes to the team. Keep it flexible, too—decide how easy or hard it is to tweak these rules later on. And, just like any game, you want to know how it ends, right? So, talk about how you'd close up shop if that ever comes up. It's basically creating a roadmap for your business journey—simple, clear, and everyone's on the same page, making sure the game runs smoothly. Instead of using an operating agreement, which is specific to an LLC, an S corporation will rely on its corporate bylaws and articles of incorporation which carry out many of the same functions.

Step 2: Choosing the Right Management Structure

CASE STUDY:

For generations, Sweet Haven, the family-owned bakery, had been a beloved local institution, known for its mouth watering pastries and warm, welcoming atmosphere. However, as the years passed, Sweet Haven began to face the challenges of a changing market and increased competition.

Amelia Turner, the owner of Sweet Haven, could sense the urgency to adapt. Determined to secure the future of her family's business, she decided to make a bold move — establishing a board of directors. This board would consist of a carefully chosen blend of existing employees and external experts.

From within the bakery, Amelia selected Jake Miller, the head pastry chef with a deep understanding of the baking process, and Lily Rodriguez, the customer service manager who had a knack for understanding the preferences of Sweet Haven's loyal customers. Their firsthand experience and dedication made them valuable contributors to the board.

Amelia also recognized the need for external perspectives to guide Sweet Haven through the modern business landscape. She invited Michael Reynolds, a marketing guru with a history of helping small businesses thrive, and Olivia Carter, a financial consultant known for her expertise in turning around struggling enterprises.

Together, this diverse board of advisors began meeting regularly to brainstorm and strategize. Jake brought insights into new pastry trends and even began offering unique coffee flavors, while Lily shared valuable feedback from customers about their experiences. Michael devised marketing campaigns that highlighted Sweet Haven's unique charm and history, and Olivia implemented financial strategies to streamline operations and cut unnecessary costs.

The board's impact was profound. Sweet Haven started to regain its position as a community favorite, with lines forming outside the bakery every morning. The board's recommendations led to the introduction of innovative pastries that appealed to a wider audience, and marketing initiatives drew in new customers while retaining the loyalty of existing ones.

As Sweet Haven flourished under the guidance of the board of advisors, Amelia felt a renewed sense of pride and accomplishment. The collaboration between the dedicated employees and the external experts proved to be the perfect recipe for success. Sweet Haven not only survived the challenges but emerged as a thriving business, blending tradition with innovation.

The story of Sweet Haven serves as a testament to the transformative power of collaboration and strategic decision-making. Amelia Turner's decision to establish a board, combining the strengths of her loyal employees with the expertise of external professionals, saved Sweet Haven from the brink of decline and ensured its continued success for generations to come.

First, it's important to know the difference between a member and a manager in an LLC. Members are like the owners—they invest money, have a say in big decisions, and are protected from the company's debts affecting their personal stuff. Managers, on the other hand, are the ones in charge of running the show day-to-day. They make the daily decisions and implement the business plan. Here's the thing: a member can also be a manager, but sometimes these roles are kept separate, especially in bigger LLCs where members might want to let someone else handle the day-to-day stuff so they elect managers that don't have any ownership. The key is to make it clear who's doing what in the LLC's operating agreement so everyone knows their role.

Many business owners opt to establish a voting board of directors when creating their operating agreements. Making decisions for your business is a big deal, and sometimes, having a group of people to help out can be a game-changer. The board can be made up of a combination of members and managers.

Let's explore the good things and the challenges that come with having a board.

Firstly, the good stuff – having a bunch of different people on your board means you get a mix of skills and experiences. This variety can really help when you're trying to figure out what's best for your business. The collective wisdom of the board can guide you through tough times and help you spot opportunities you might have missed. Plus, having a board can make your business look more trustworthy to investors and other important people.

But, of course, there are challenges too. Having a bunch of people making decisions together can sometimes lead to conflicts. People might not always agree, and that can slow things down. Also, forming a board takes time and effort. Meetings, discussions, and planning sessions can take up a lot of everyone's schedule. And for business owners used to calling all the shots, it might be tough to share the decision-making power.

Tamela and I recommend having an uneven number of people on a board to avoid potential ties or deadlocks when voting on decisions. When there's an odd number of board members, it ensures that there will always be a clear majority or a decisive outcome in voting situations. In a scenario where the board is evenly split between two options, it could lead to challenges in making important decisions, and breaking the tie may be difficult. Having an odd number, such as three, five, seven, etc., helps prevent this situation and enables the board to reach more definitive resolutions.

Despite these challenges, having a well-thought-out board usually brings more benefits. It's like having a team that brings fresh ideas, helps you avoid risks, and ensures your business lasts a long time. It's often a smart move that can take your business to new heights.

CASE STUDY:

This is the story of a successful trucking company known as Horizon Logistics, owned by an entrepreneur named James Anderson. Despite the company's thriving business, James realized the potential for expansion and improvement. To navigate this journey, he decided to form a board of directors, seeking individuals who could bring diverse skills to the table.

Among the carefully selected board members was Rachel Regan, an experienced financial adviser renowned for her ability to secure funding and provide strategic financial guidance. As the board of directors convened, James shared his vision of taking Horizon Logistics to new heights by constructing a modern logistics hub that could efficiently handle the growing demands of the industry.

Rachel, armed with her financial expertise, delved into the company's financial standing and future projections. Presenting her findings to the board, she proposed a comprehensive plan to secure the necessary financing for the construction of the new logistics center.

Impressed by Rachel's strategic approach, the board unanimously approved her proposal. With the financial backing secured, Horizon Logistics embarked on an ambitious journey to build its cutting-edge logistics hub, equipped with state-of-the-art facilities and advanced technology.

Throughout the construction phase, Rachel continued to play a pivotal role, advising the board on financial strategies to optimize the company's growth. Her insights helped Horizon Logistics navigate economic challenges in the trucking industry and make informed decisions that maximized profitability.

Under the guidance of the board of directors, Horizon Logistics flourished. The new logistics hub became a beacon of efficiency and innovation in the transportation sector. The company attracted top talent, formed strategic partnerships, and expanded its services across new territories.

James Anderson, with the support of the dedicated board and Rachel's financial expertise, witnessed Horizon Logistics not only reaching the next level but becoming a leader in the trucking industry. The success story of Horizon Logistics served as inspiration for others in the transportation business, highlighting the transformative power of strategic leadership and financial expertise in an ever-evolving industry.

Adding outside experts to a business's board of directors is a smart move for a few key reasons. First off, these experts bring in fresh and unbiased perspectives. Financial advisers can help with money matters, ensuring the company's finances are in good shape, while industry experts can guide the business through the latest trends. Secondly, having a diverse group of experts improves the ability to solve problems creatively and makes the business more innovative. Third, these external experts bring a wealth of experience, offering valuable advice on tricky issues and helping the company make better decisions. In a nutshell, having outside experts on the board can make a business smarter, more efficient, and better equipped for long-term success.

The decision to establish a board of directors will differ for every business and owner. On the positive side, having a board with different experts and viewpoints can give really helpful advice, smart strategies, and creative solutions. It's like having a powerful team to guide the business through tough times and help it succeed in the long run. But, it's important to recognize the possible downsides, like more paperwork, potential conflicts, and the need for clear communication. So, the trick is to think carefully and plan strategically before deciding whether a board is the right move for the business.

Step 3: Financial Foundations

CASE STUDY:

The minds behind Serenity Homes were Adrian and Olivia Sterling. Serenity Homes flourished, raking in an impressive 19 million dollars in revenue during its third year in business. The Sterlings were known for their commitment to delivering homes of exceptional quality, and the demand for their services soared. However, unbeknownst to the outside world, a critical aspect of their business was slowly unraveling.

Adrian and Olivia, deeply passionate about the art of construction, poured their energy into the creative and operational aspects of their projects. Regrettably, they neglected a pivotal component: maintaining meticulous financial records. As the company expanded, so did the complexities of its financial transactions.

The absence of proper bookkeeping became the Achilles' heel of Serenity Homes. The founders were unaware of the areas where they were making profits and where they were hemorrhaging money. Without accurate financial insights, they couldn't identify inefficiencies, control costs, or make informed strategic decisions.

Projects were initiated without a clear understanding of their profitability, subcontractors were hired without thorough cost analysis, and expenses were managed without a comprehensive budget. The lack of financial transparency led to a series of unfortunate events that ultimately sealed the fate of Serenity Homes.

The construction industry, renowned for its cutthroat nature, began to take its toll on the company. Unbeknownst to Adrian and Olivia, some projects were draining resources without yielding the anticipated returns. While they were busy chasing new contracts, existing projects were slipping through the cracks, both financially and in terms of quality control.

As financial discrepancies piled up, Serenity Homes found itself in a precarious position. The company struggled to meet its financial obligations, and creditors started knocking on the door. Despite their best efforts to salvage the business, Adrian and Olivia were forced to make the heart-wrenching decision to close the doors of Serenity Homes.

The downfall of the once-thriving company served as a cautionary tale for entrepreneurs in the construction industry. Adrian and Olivia learned a valuable lesson about the importance of financial management and the need to keep accurate and up-to-date records. The legacy they had hoped to build crumbled not due to a lack of skill or passion for construction but rather because they underestimated the significance of understanding the financial health of their business.

And so, the city of Crestfield witnessed the rise and fall of Serenity Homes, a tale of success overshadowed by the consequences of neglecting the crucial discipline of keeping good books.

Maintaining accurate financial records is critical. The foundation for informed decision-making lies in accurate financial records which provide a complete view of a company's financial health. It's simply not possible for a business to make good management decisions without accurate accounting.

Accounts receivable (AR) is the money owed to a business by its customers. Efficient tracking and management of accounts receivable are essential for maintaining a healthy cash flow. Timely invoicing, clear credit terms, and effective communication with customers are key factors that contribute to minimizing late payments. This, in turn, ensures that the business has the cash needed to meet its obligations and pursue growth opportunities.

On the other side of the financial spectrum, accounts payable (AP) refers to the money a business owes to its suppliers and creditors. Managing accounts payable effectively is vital for maintaining positive relationships with vendors and avoiding late payment penalties. Accurate financial records provide the visibility needed to track and organize payables, ensuring that the business meets its financial obligations in a timely manner. This not only fosters goodwill with suppliers but also contributes to a smooth and sustainable supply chain.

Beyond tracking inflows and outflows, businesses must identify how profitable different areas of their business are. Accurate financial records facilitate an analysis of revenue streams, expenses, and profit margins, helping identify areas of excellence and those that may need help. Financial records aid in the allocation of costs to specific products, services, or departments. This detailed view enables businesses to identify profitable offerings and strategically allocate resources, contributing to effective cost management and pricing strategies.

Meticulous record-keeping allows businesses to identify trends and patterns in financial performance. This dynamic understanding aids in recognizing seasonal fluctuations, identifying the impact of marketing initiatives, and making proactive adjustments to optimize profitability. It will also help pinpoint aspects of the business experiencing losses. This insight allows for swift responses, such as implementing cost-cutting measures or reevaluating strategies to turn around underperforming segments.

Accurate financial records empower business leaders with insights for strategic decision-making. Whether scaling successful operations, diversifying offerings, or discontinuing unprofitable ventures, informed decisions contribute to long-term sustainability.

CASE STUDY:

Ezra, a creative soul with a passion for print and design, poured his heart into Luminary Press. As the sole owner, he handled everything from design to customer service. However, behind the scenes, Ezra grappled with the financial management of his business. Fearing the complexities of modern accounting software like QuickBooks and the costs associated with professional bookkeeping services, he chose to manage his finances manually.

As Luminary Press gained popularity, so did the intricacies of its financial records. Ezra, fueled by determination, spent countless hours navigating through a labyrinth of receipts and spreadsheets. His focus on creating beautiful prints for his customers remained steadfast, but the absence of a proper accounting system began to cast a shadow on the success of Luminary Press.

One day, a friend, and local pastor named Pastor James, paid a visit to Luminary Press. Observing Ezra's struggle, he gently reminded him of the importance of being a good steward of the resources that God had provided. Drawing inspiration from Biblical teachings on responsible stewardship, Pastor James encouraged Ezra to reconsider his approach to financial management.

Recognizing the wisdom in the pastor's words, Ezra decided to embrace change. He acknowledged the need to implement QuickBooks to streamline his financial processes. To his surprise, the software proved to be more user-friendly than he had anticipated, dispelling his initial concerns about complexity and cost.

With accurate financial records at his fingertips, Luminary Press gained valuable insights into its financial health. Ezra could now make informed decisions, refine pricing strategies, and identify areas for business improvement. As a result, Luminary Press not only survived but flourished once more, with the continued support of the community.

In the end, the story of Luminary Press and its unique owner, Ezra Hawthorne, became a testament to the significance of responsible stewardship and the willingness to adapt to tools that enhance the management of God's blessings. Ezra learned that embracing change and seeking assistance when necessary were pivotal steps in ensuring the sustained success of his entrusted gift.

Keeping good books is not an option for businesses—it's a necessity. Every business, big or small, must take the necessary steps to maintain accurate records of their finances. Proper bookkeeping, whether through tools like QuickBooks or professional services, ensures that a business understands its income, expenses, and overall financial health. Without accurate records, businesses will undoubtedly face challenges in making informed decisions, understanding their profitability, and navigating the complexities of cash flow. This should be a priority for every business.

Here's a list of priorities for business bookkeeping:

1. Record Transactions: Ensure all financial transactions, including sales, purchases, expenses, and payments, are accurately recorded in the accounting system.

2. Invoice and Receipt Management: Create and track invoices for sales, and keep records of receipts for all expenses. This helps in maintaining a clear trail of financial activities.

3. Bank Reconciliation: Regularly reconcile bank statements with the business accounts to identify any discrepancies and ensure that the recorded transactions match the actual bank transactions.

4. Expense Tracking: Categorize and track all business expenses. This includes fixed costs like rent and utilities, as well as variable costs like office supplies and travel expenses.

5. Payroll Management: If applicable, accurately manage payroll, including tracking hours worked, calculating taxes, and ensuring timely payment to employees.

6. Financial Reporting: Generate frequent financial reports such as income statements, balance sheets, and cash flow statements. These reports provide insights into the financial health of the business and will keep you on track.

7. Tax Compliance: Stay updated on tax regulations and ensure timely filing of all required tax returns. Keep records of all tax-related documents.

8. Audit Preparation: Maintain organized financial records to facilitate audits if required. This includes keeping receipts, invoices, and supporting documents for transactions.

9. Budgeting and Forecasting: Develop and monitor a budget for the business, comparing actual financial performance against budgeted figures. Forecast future financial needs and plan accordingly.

10. Asset and Depreciation Tracking: Keep track of the company's assets, their value, and depreciation. This is crucial for accurate financial reporting and tax calculations.

11. Vendor and Customer Management: Keep accurate records of transactions with vendors and customers. This includes payment terms, outstanding invoices, and any credit terms.

12. Compliance with Regulations: Ensure compliance with relevant financial regulations and industry standards. This may include accounting standards, industry-specific regulations, and any other legal requirements.

13. Financial Software Maintenance: Regularly update and maintain accounting software to ensure it meets the business's needs and stays compatible with any changes in regulations.

14. Cash Flow Management: Monitor and manage cash flow to ensure there is enough liquidity to cover expenses and investments.

15. Regular Reviews: Conduct regular reviews of financial records to identify any errors, discrepancies, or areas for improvement in the bookkeeping process.

QuickBooks is a popular small business accounting software, but there are other alternatives in the market, each with its own set of pros and cons. Additionally, there are industry-specific solutions tailored to the needs of specific businesses. QuickBooks stands out for its user-friendly interface, comprehensive features, and scalability, accommodating both small and growing enterprises. However, some users find it relatively expensive, and there might be a learning curve for those new to accounting software. Alternatives like Xero and FreshBooks offer unique strengths, such as real-time collaboration and intuitive interfaces, but may have different learning curves and customization options. Additionally, industry-specific solutions like Zoho Books (for service-based businesses), QuickBooks Online Advanced (for retail), and Sage 50 cloud (for construction) cater to specific business needs but may lack the versatility of more general accounting software. Ultimately, the choice depends on factors such as business size, industry, required features, and budget. Exploring trial versions or demos can help in making an informed decision based on the business's unique requirements.

When deciding between in-house bookkeeping and hiring an agency, you need to consider various factors. In-house bookkeeping offers cost control, immediate access to information, and customization but can be time-consuming and may require expertise. Hiring an agency brings expertise and time savings, making it suitable for focusing on core activities, but comes with costs and external dependency. The choice depends on factors like business size, budget, expertise, time commitment, regulatory compliance, and technology requirements. Some businesses choose a hybrid approach, combining in-house bookkeeping for daily tasks with periodic reviews by external agencies. Ultimately, the decision should align with your business priorities, financial capabilities, and growth plans.

It's important to understand the distinction between a bookkeeper and a certified public accountant (CPA). A bookkeeper typically handles day-to-day financial tasks, such as recording transactions, managing invoices, and reconciling accounts. Bookkeepers are valuable for maintaining accurate and up-to-date financial records. On the other hand, a certified public accountant (CPA) is a licensed professional with advanced training in accounting and taxation. CPAs can provide higher-level financial services, including tax planning, auditing, and financial analysis. Use a bookkeeper when you need regular, routine financial tasks managed efficiently. When facing complex financial challenges, tax-related issues, or the need for strategic financial planning, it's advisable to engage a CPA. While bookkeepers and CPAs play different roles, collaborating with both can create a robust financial management system for your business.

Step 4:

Borrowing Money

Businesses often rely on borrowing money for growth, projects, or financial challenges. However, it's crucial to be strategic and avoid high-interest bridge loans, which can lead to financial strain. Exploring alternative lending options and carefully assessing terms will help a business make informed decisions.

A bridge loan is a short-term financing option designed to provide immediate funds until a more permanent financing solution is secured. While bridge loans can offer quick access to capital, they often come with high-interest rates and fees, making them a less favorable option for businesses. The high costs associated with bridge loans can significantly impact a company's financial health, potentially leading to increased debt and financial strain. Businesses considering bridge loans should be cautious of the potential long-term consequences and explore alternative financing options with more favorable terms to avoid the pitfalls of high-interest bridge loans. Bridge loans should be avoided if at all possible.

CASE STUDY:

Green Bins Disposal, a trash collection company, was faced with sudden financial challenges and needed immediate funds to cover their weekly payroll. Green Bins opted for a bridge loan with a staggering 36% interest rate. The decision seemed urgent and the loan seemed like a promising fix to their cash flow woes.

As the months passed, the burden of the high-interest bridge loan began to take its toll on Green Bins. Despite their efforts to meet the hefty monthly payments, the mounting interest became unsustainable. The company found itself caught in a vicious cycle, struggling to keep up with the financial obligations imposed by the bridge loan. Some months the company had to take out another bridge loan just to offset the damage from the high interest rates.

Despite their essential service to the community, the weight of the debt proved too much for Green Bins Disposal. The soaring interest rates, coupled with the business's inability to secure more favorable financing, eventually led to their downfall. Green Bins, once a reliable trash collection service, had to shutter its operations, leaving employees without jobs and the community without a vital service.

The tale of Green Bins Disposal serves as a cautionary reminder of the perils associated with high-interest bridge loans. While the promise of quick cash may seem enticing in the short term, the long-term consequences can be devastating for businesses. It underscores the importance of carefully evaluating financing options, considering the impact of interest rates, and exploring alternatives to ensure the sustainability and success of the business in the long run.

The easiest way for a business to build credit is by establishing and nurturing relationships with a reputable bank. A positive and longstanding association with a good bank can significantly contribute to a business's creditworthiness. By maintaining consistent and timely transactions, such as making loan payments and managing accounts responsibly, a business demonstrates financial responsibility to the bank. This, in turn, can lead to increased trust and a positive credit history. Building a strong relationship with a reliable bank not only supports the day-to-day financial operations of the business but also plays a pivotal role in establishing a favorable credit profile, making it easier to access financing options with competitive terms in the future.

CPAs play a vital role in helping businesses secure loans. They assist in preparing accurate financial statements, budgets, and forecasts, providing lenders with a clear view of the business's financial health. CPAs also offer guidance on financial management practices and tax planning, instilling confidence in lenders.

Moreover, CPAs help identify suitable financing options and navigate the lending landscape. Whether it's a term loan or a line of credit, their expertise ensures businesses make informed decisions. With a strategic approach to borrowing and the guidance of a CPA, businesses can secure financing and make choices that contribute to long-term financial success.

Having a CPA stamp your financials adds significant value to a company's financial statements. When financial statements are prepared and reviewed by a CPA, it instills a high level of credibility and reliability. The stamp of a CPA indicates that the statements have undergone a rigorous examination, ensuring accuracy and adherence to accounting standards. This level of assurance is particularly valuable for businesses seeking external financing, as lenders and investors often place greater trust in financial statements that bear the mark of a qualified CPA. Moreover, CPA-stamped financials enhance transparency and build confidence among stakeholders, including shareholders, regulators, and potential business partners. The stamp signifies a commitment to financial integrity, making it a valuable asset for businesses navigating the complex landscape of financial reporting and decision-making.

Selecting the right business loan is a crucial decision that requires careful consideration. Here are key things to look for when choosing a business loan.

1. Interest Rates: Look for competitive interest rates. Lower rates can significantly reduce the overall cost of the loan.

2. Fees and Charges: Be aware of any fees associated with the loan, such as origination fees, application fees, and prepayment penalties. Transparent fee structures are a must.

3. Total Cost of Capital: Evaluate the total cost of capital, which includes both interest rates and fees. Understanding the overall expense ensures an accurate comparison between different loan options.

4. Early Repayment Options: Check if there are penalties for early repayment. Some loans charge fees if you pay off the loan before the agreed-upon term.

5. Loan Amount: Ensure the loan amount meets your business's financing needs. Avoid borrowing more than necessary to prevent unnecessary interest costs.

6. Security and Collateral: Understand the collateral requirements. Secured loans may offer lower interest rates but involve putting assets at risk.

7. Loan Purpose: Some loans are designed for specific purposes (e.g., equipment loans, working capital loans). Choose a loan aligned with your business needs.

8. Flexibility: Assess the flexibility of the loan. Business lines of credit, for example, offer flexibility in drawing funds as needed.

9. Qualification Criteria: Understand the qualification criteria. Some loans may have stringent eligibility requirements, and it's essential to ensure your business meets them.

10. Lender Reputation: Research the reputation of the lender. Look for reviews, testimonials, and the lender's track record in serving businesses.

11. Speed of Approval and Funding: Consider the time it takes for approval and funding.

12. Government-Backed Options: Explore government-backed loan programs, such as SBA loans, which often offer favorable terms for small businesses.

13. Customer Support: Assess the quality of customer support. A responsive and helpful lender can make the loan process smoother.

14. Terms and Conditions: Carefully read and understand all terms and conditions in the loan agreement. Seek clarification on any unclear points.

15. Credit Score Impact: Understand how the loan may impact your credit score. Regular, timely payments can positively influence your credit standing.

16. Industry Experience: Some lenders specialize in specific industries. Choosing a lender familiar with your industry can be advantageous.

17. Legal and Regulatory Compliance: Ensure the lender complies with legal and regulatory requirements. Verify their licensing and adherence to industry standards.

CASE STUDY:

Jim and Lisa Thompson had spent over a decade pouring their hearts into the charming campground they owned. Tucked away in the scenic hills, their slice of nature had become a beloved retreat for families and outdoor enthusiasts. However, as the years passed, the Thompsons sensed a shift in the industry, and they recognized the need for a breath of fresh air to keep their campground thriving.

One evening, after the last campfire had dwindled to embers, Jim turned to Lisa with a spark in his eye. "Imagine if we could add a splash pad by the lake and a bouncing pillow near the playground. Families would love it, and it would make us much more competitive in the region."

Lisa, always the pragmatic one, nodded thoughtfully. "But we'll need to invest in these upgrades. What if we took out a loan to fund these improvements and more? We could make our campground a top-tier destination but it can be risky."

Excitement filled the air as they sketched out plans for a modern playground, a splash pad with vibrant water features, a bouncing pillow and even a new camp store. However, the couple knew they needed more than enthusiasm; they needed strategic guidance.

Enter Sarah Morgan, a financial expert and avid camper, who shared their passion for the great outdoors. The Thompsons approached Sarah with a proposition: join their venture as a partner and help steer the business toward a brighter future. Sarah, intrigued by the idea of merging her financial expertise with her love for camping, eagerly accepted.

Together, they decided to formalize their collaboration by forming a board of directors. In addition to the Thompsons and Sarah, they invited Mark Reynolds, a marketing whiz, and Emily Adams, a hospitality veteran, to join the team. The diverse backgrounds of the board members promised a well-rounded approach to decision-making.

The newly formed board wasted no time. They conducted a thorough analysis of market trends, customer preferences, and financial projections. Sarah, drawing on her financial acumen, helped the Thompsons understand the risks and rewards associated with taking out a loan. They weighed the potential return on investment for each proposed improvement, ensuring they were making informed decisions for the future of the campground.

With a comprehensive business plan in hand, they approached financial institutions to secure a loan. Sarah's expertise was instrumental in presenting a compelling case to lenders, and soon enough, they secured the funds needed to turn their dreams into reality.

Construction began on the splash pad, bouncing pillow, and playground upgrades. The board of directors continued to meet regularly, providing ongoing insights and strategies to enhance the campground's appeal. As the improvements took shape, word spread, and families from far and wide started making reservations.

The campground experienced a resurgence, attracting a diverse clientele. Jim and Lisa beamed with pride as they saw children gleefully playing on the bouncing pillow, families enjoying the new splash pad, and campers reveling in the upgraded facilities.

The collaboration between the Thompsons and their new partners proved to be a winning formula. The campground, once at risk of losing its charm, had transformed into a vibrant destination, thanks to the strategic vision of the board of directors and the financial expertise of Sarah. Together, they not only secured the future of the campground but also created a haven where families could create lasting memories in the heart of nature.

When considering a business loan, it's crucial to start with a clear understanding of your company's finances. Take a close look at factors such as cash flow, revenue projections, and overall financial stability. This not only helps determine the amount you need but also demonstrates to lenders that you're informed and capable of managing funds responsibly. Knowing your financial position enables you to create a realistic repayment plan, ensuring you don't take on more debt than your business can handle.

Developing a detailed business plan is just as important in the loan-seeking process. Lenders want to see a clear roadmap outlining how the borrowed funds will be used to improve the business and generate returns. A well-thought-out plan with specific goals, timelines, and financial projections serves as a persuasive tool for lenders and a practical guide for your business strategies. Additionally, researching the best loan options and partnering with financial experts can be key in securing favorable terms. Financial advisors offer valuable insights into different loan products, help decipher financial jargon, and assist in finding the most suitable financing solution for your business needs. This collaborative approach ensures that the decision to take a business loan is well-informed, strategic, and contributes positively to the long-term success of the enterprise.

Step 5:
Building a Strong Team

Building a strong team for your business is a step-by-step process. Start by defining your company's values and goals. Ask yourself why you have chosen the business that you have and take the time to formalize these ideas in a well thought out document. This sets the tone and ensures everyone is on the same page. Once you know what you're looking for, create job descriptions that clearly outline the skills and expectations for each role.

When it's time to pick people for your team, have a plan for interviews. Ask questions that help you understand how well the applicant can solve problems and collaborate. It's imperative to have a well thought through and organized interview process. Being organized will help you identify the right candidate and leave them with a great first impression. The interviewee should leave with the impression that you are organized and ready to train them in their new role.

CASE STUDY:

A small and struggling cell phone repair shop called TechRevive was struggling to find skilled technicians who shared their dedication to quality and customer satisfaction. Determined to turn things around, the owner decided to revamp their hiring process. They started by redefining their job descriptions. Instead of solely emphasizing technical skills, they highlighted the importance of customer service, attention to detail, and problem-solving abilities. They wanted candidates who not only knew their way around a smartphone but also understood the value of a satisfied customer.

The interview process underwent a transformation as well. Instead of the typical one-on-one interviews, TechRevive implemented a practical approach. Candidates were given repair scenarios to assess their technical skills, but they were also evaluated on how well they communicated with potential clients. This team-based interview approach allowed Alex and Maria to ensure that new hires not only had the technical expertise but also the interpersonal skills crucial for customer interactions.

TechRevive introduced a hands-on skills assessment phase to the hiring process. Candidates were presented with damaged phones and asked to diagnose and repair them. This step not only demonstrated the candidates' technical proficiency but also their ability to handle the real-world challenges that often arose in the repair business.

Transparency became a key focus of TechRevive's new hiring strategy. The owner believed in setting clear expectations about the work environment, the importance of customer satisfaction, and the potential for growth within the company. This approach not only attracted candidates genuinely interested in providing quality service but also fostered a sense of trust from the very beginning.

As TechRevive implemented these changes, the results were remarkable. The shop began to attract skilled technicians who not only excelled at repairing devices but also valued customer relationships. The team's cohesion improved, creating an environment where collaboration and knowledge-sharing became the norm.

Word spread about TechRevive's exceptional hiring process, and soon, the shop became known as the go-to place for not only phone repairs but also as a great workplace. Skilled technicians sought out opportunities to join the team, bringing their expertise and enthusiasm for customer service.

The situational interview process is highly effective and should be a part of every hiring plan. It involves presenting candidates with hypothetical scenarios or real-world situations relevant to the job they are applying for. The goal is to evaluate how candidates would handle specific challenges or tasks, assessing their problem-solving skills, decision-making abilities, and practical application of knowledge.

For instance, consider a scenario in hiring a project manager. A situational interview question could be: "You are leading a project with tight deadlines, and a key team member unexpectedly resigns. How would you handle this situation to ensure the project stays on track?" Here, the candidate is expected to articulate their approach, addressing issues like reallocating responsibilities, communicating with stakeholders, and maintaining team morale.

This type of interview allows employers to assess not only a candidate's theoretical knowledge but also their ability to think critically, devise practical solutions, and demonstrate interpersonal and leadership skills in response to real-world challenges. It goes beyond assessing what a candidate knows and focuses on how they would apply their knowledge in the dynamic and unpredictable nature of the job.

The situational interview process offers several advantages in candidate evaluation. It allows employers to assess how candidates would apply their skills in practical, job-related scenarios, providing a more accurate measure of problem-solving and decision-making abilities. This method is particularly valuable for roles requiring quick thinking and adaptability.

Moreover, the situational interview helps predict future job performance by evaluating a candidate's response to realistic challenges. It offers insights into thought processes, problem-solving strategies, and alignment with organizational values. This understanding contributes to more informed hiring decisions.

Integrating the situational interview with the group interview format enhances the evaluation process. In a group setting, candidates are observed for both individual responses to challenges and teamwork skills. This dual approach provides a holistic view, assessing both individual competencies and the ability to collaborate within a team. It simulates workplace dynamics, revealing how candidates contribute to group problem-solving and decision-making.

Consider the following when developing interview questions and scenarios:

Adaptability and Learning Agility: In a rapidly evolving work environment, the ability to adapt and learn quickly is essential. Assess a candidate's openness to change, ability to acquire new skills, and willingness to embrace challenges.

Emotional Intelligence: Evaluate a candidate's emotional intelligence, including their self-awareness, empathy, and interpersonal skills. This is especially important for roles requiring effective collaboration, leadership, or client interactions.

Problem-Solving Approach: Understand how candidates approach problem-solving. Assess their creativity, analytical thinking, and resourcefulness, as these qualities can be indicative of their ability to overcome challenges on the job.

Resilience and Stress Management: Explore how candidates handle stress and setbacks. Resilience is crucial in dynamic work environments, and individuals who can maintain composure and productivity under pressure are often valuable assets to a team.

Communication Skills: Effective communication extends beyond verbal articulation. Evaluate a candidate's written communication skills, as well as their ability to convey complex ideas in a clear and concise manner, which is essential for effective collaboration.

Long-Term Career Goals: Discuss the candidate's long-term career aspirations to ensure alignment with the company's growth trajectory. This consideration helps identify candidates who view the role as a strategic step in their career path.

Ethical Decision-Making: Assess a candidate's ethical decision-making process. Present scenarios that touch on ethical considerations relevant to the role to gauge their values and integrity, which are integral to maintaining a positive workplace culture.

Work-Life Balance Expectations: Openly discuss work-life balance expectations to ensure mutual understanding. Understanding a candidate's priorities outside of work can contribute to a healthier work environment and long-term employee satisfaction.

CASE STUDY:

Michael, the owner of a marketing firm, was determined to redefine the hiring experience for his creative team. Dissatisfied with the predictability of traditional interviews, Michael decided to infuse innovation into his hiring process by implementing the situational interview process – complete with props.

Turning a section of his office into an imaginative brainstorming room, Michael set the stage for a dynamic interview experience. As candidates entered, they encountered an array of props ranging from marketing collateral mock-ups to interactive digital displays. The situational interviews were now a hands-on exploration of a candidate's ability to tackle real-world marketing challenges.

One candidate, Emily, a seasoned content strategist, found herself faced with a quirky collection of brand elements – logos, taglines, and visuals. Michael challenged her to create an impromptu marketing campaign for a fictional product using the provided elements. Emily dove into the task with enthusiasm, showcasing not only her creativity but also her strategic thinking in crafting a cohesive and compelling brand narrative.

In another interview, John, a candidate for a project management role, was presented with a scenario involving a jigsaw puzzle representing a complex marketing campaign. Michael asked him to discuss how he would organize and coordinate the various pieces to ensure a seamless execution. As John maneuvered through the puzzle, he articulated a strategic plan, showcasing his organizational skills and ability to navigate intricate projects.

The props added an element of excitement to the interviews, sparking candid conversations about candidates' creative processes and problem-solving approaches. Michael observed how candidates embraced the challenges with enthusiasm, providing valuable insights into their adaptability and hands-on marketing capabilities.

As the interviews concluded, Michael couldn't help but feel a sense of accomplishment. The situational interview process with props not only unearthed the technical expertise of the candidates but also revealed their passion for innovation and ability to bring marketing concepts to life. Word quickly spread about Michael's inventive approach, and his marketing firm became known for attracting top talent that not only possessed the requisite skills but also embodied the creativity and agility needed in the ever-evolving world of marketing. Michael's innovative hiring strategy became a hallmark of the firm's success, ensuring a dynamic and vibrant team that continued to push the boundaries of marketing excellence.

When developing an interview process for your small business, don't be afraid to get creative! Instead of sticking to traditional methods, think outside the box. Adding a touch of creativity can help you discover unique skills and see how well candidates adapt to different situations. Try using interesting questions or practical exercises that mirror real work scenarios. This not only makes the process more engaging but also gives you a better idea of whether the candidate is a good fit for the role. Being creative in your interviews can break down barriers, allowing for a more genuine connection and setting the stage for a positive and productive work environment.

Once your team is formed, invest in their growth. Provide training and mentorship to help each member reach their full potential. Creating a training program will be time consuming and require an investment. There are many online resources to help you get started but first you have to decide on the training format that will work best for your business. You will need to choose between video training, classroom training, apprenticeships, or a combination of the three. Video training can be highly effective and save you time and money over time but will require you to create thorough and interesting videos in the beginning.

Despite efforts, sometimes a team member may not be the right fit. It's a tough decision, but if someone isn't contributing positively, consider making changes. One employee can ruin the experience for the entire team and create an unwelcoming work environment. As an owner or manager it can be difficult to terminate an employee. Just like you developed an interview process to hire, you should take the time to develop a process to release an employee. This can make things much less stressful for both you and the employee. It's about maintaining the overall health of the team.

Lastly, focus on continuous improvement. Regularly discuss what's working well and what needs adjustment. This ongoing process ensures your team remains adaptable and thrives over time.

Step 6:
Marketing and Branding

Creating a successful marketing plan for your small business involves a few key principles. One important idea is "multi-touch marketing," which means reaching potential customers through different channels. However, it's crucial for small businesses to be smart about spending money on this method. Budgeting carefully helps make sure that the money spent on marketing brings in more profits.

Sometimes, business owners can be tricked into spending a lot on multi-touch marketing strategies that promise big results, but there's no clear way to know if they actually work. This can happen because owners may feel pressured to keep up with competitors or fear they'll miss out on potential opportunities. Clever marketers might tell convincing stories without providing real proof of success. The idea of reaching customers through different channels can seem appealing, but it's important for business owners to stay cautious. Asking for concrete evidence, like trackable numbers or success stories, can help make sure they're not falling for tricks. Being careful and checking the facts can protect business owners and make sure their marketing money is well spent.

CASE STUDY:

A budding solar energy company named SunGlow found itself at a crossroads. Eager to increase its market presence, SunGlow entered into a contract with a flashy marketing firm. They promised the world with their multi-touch marketing services, claiming it would skyrocket SunGlow's sales and brand recognition. The only catch was the hefty price tag attached to the contract, a sum that made SunGlow's leadership skeptical.

Despite reservations about the cost, the owner of SunGlow was optimistic and hopeful that the marketing firm's expertise would be a game-changer. The contract was signed, and the marketing campaign kicked off with a dazzling array of beautifully crafted imagery —from social media blitzes to high-profile events. SunGlow's logo was plastered everywhere, and the company eagerly anticipated the influx of customers.

As time passed, however, the results were not as promising as they had been promised. The increased brand visibility did not translate into a proportional uptick in sales, and the once hopeful atmosphere at SunGlow started to dim. The financial strain from the exorbitant marketing costs began to weigh heavily on the company's bottom line, leaving them struggling to recover.

In the aftermath of this marketing misadventure, SunGlow's leadership learned a valuable lesson. They realized the importance of directing their marketing budget toward verifiable and trackable strategies that could guarantee a return on investment. SunGlow made a strategic shift, focusing on measuring outcomes by tracking customer acquisition costs, and conversion rates. By embracing a data-driven approach, they were able to make informed decisions and allocate their resources more effectively.

Ultimately, SunGlow emerged from this experience wiser and more resilient. They transformed their marketing strategy, leveraging analytics and tangible metrics to guide their decisions. The tale of SunGlow serves as a cautionary reminder for businesses to prioritize trackable and verifiable marketing strategies, ensuring that their investments yield real and measurable results.

While multi-touch marketing can be powerful, small businesses need to be mindful of their limited budget. Instead of spreading money too thin across various channels, focus on the most effective ones. Prioritize channels that match your target audience and business goals. This way, you can get the most out of your marketing strategy without spending too much.

Tracking the performance of your marketing efforts is essential. Use tools and platforms to monitor how well your campaigns are doing. This data-driven approach helps you see what's working and what's not. It allows you to adjust your strategy to get the best results, ensuring that your marketing budget is well spent.

Knowing your audience is a big part of a successful marketing strategy. Understand the demographics, preferences, and behaviors of your ideal customers. This helps you tailor your messages to what they care about, increasing the chances of connecting with them.

Consistency is also key. Make sure your brand messaging, visuals, and tone stay the same across different places where customers might see you. This builds trust and recognition, making it more likely that people will remember and choose your business.

CASE STUDY:

Hunt & Gear Outfitters was a hub for outdoor enthusiasts. As the store sought to modernize its operations, they realized that their outdated phone system was holding them back from reaching their full potential. Determined to take a leap into the future, the store decided to invest in a cutting-edge voice over IP (VoIP) system.

The new VoIP system not only provided crystal-clear communication but also came with a game-changing feature for the marketing team. Instead of using a single phone number for all their advertisements, they could now generate unique phone numbers for each marketing campaign. This meant that every billboard, magazine ad, and social media post had its own dedicated phone number.

The store's marketing team seized this opportunity to associate each advertisement with a specific customer, allowing them to track the return on investment for every campaign. As a result, they could now precisely measure the success of each ad in terms of customer inquiries and purchases. This granular level of data was a revelation for the marketing team.

Armed with insights from the new system, Hunt & Gear Outfitters could easily identify which ads were hitting the bullseye and which were missing the mark. Ads that failed to generate significant interest were swiftly eliminated, freeing up resources for more impactful campaigns. The store could now allocate their marketing budget with surgical precision, ensuring that every dollar spent contributed to a measurable return on investment.

The impact of this technological upgrade was significant. The store not only witnessed a surge in customer engagement but also experienced a boost in sales.

Conclusion

Adapting to changes in business is like navigating a constantly shifting landscape. To build a resilient foundation, start with a solid operating agreement and keep accurate financial records.

Tamela and I want to express our heartfelt thanks to each and every one of you, our readers. We appreciate the time you've spent delving into the stories and lessons we've shared here. We sincerely hope you've found our experiences and insights helpful as you navigate the world of business.

Our goal has been to provide you with real-world stories and practical lessons that resonate with the ups and downs of entrepreneurship. The Graves' wish is simple: that the tales and principles in this book become tools for your own journey in business. They hope you feel inspired, motivated, and equipped with strategies to move your ventures forward. Whether you're facing challenges or celebrating victories, may the experiences shared here be a source of encouragement, innovation, and resilience.

So, thank you for joining us on this adventure. It is our genuine hope that the lessons learned in these pages stick with you and help you grow your business. As you move forward, adapt these insights to your own situation, and may your future endeavors be filled with growth, satisfaction, and lasting success. God bless you!

We genuinely value the community we've built through this book and would love to hear from you online. Whether you're facing specific challenges, have questions about the insights shared, or simply want to share your own business story, we invite you to connect with us. Your experiences matter, and we believe that learning and growing together makes for a stronger business.

Feel free to reach out through our website or social media platforms. We cherish the opportunity to engage with readers, offering guidance, support, and a friendly ear for your business endeavors. Your questions and stories are not just welcome; they are the heartbeat of this community. So, don't hesitate to connect – let's continue this conversation!

www.rescueconsultants.com

www.ingramcontent.com/pod-product-compliance
Lightning Source LLC
Chambersburg PA
CBHW071434220526
45469CB00004B/1533